Own Your Influence

An Unconventional Journey to Making an Impact at Work

Sherenne Simon

ISBN 979-8-9903091-7-3 hardcover

ISBN 979-8-9903091-1-1 paperback

ISBN 979-8-9903091-2-8 ebook

Cover Artwork by Pandalogue Design

Cover Photo by Jordana Sheara

Published by ChromaBloom Books

Contact: ChromaBloomBooks@gmail.com

To my mom, I love you as high as the sky...

Contents

Introduction

It's Saturday morning, and I'm trying to psych myself up for the task of the day: updating my resume. Ugh...you've all been there. Procrastination wins. I go to the gym, do a load of laundry, scroll through Instagram, and hang with my family as the hours tick by. When I eventually sit down at my desk, I'm stuck. It's never easy to capture hard work, blood, sweat, and tears in a series of bullet points with a tone of professionalism. This time, I really have no idea what to say. How do I express: *I did something truly amazing and left a legacy?* How do I share that *I changed a $100 million organization with one email* in one or two measly sentences?

Guess what? I can't. It's not possible.

I wrote this book because, honestly, people do amazing things at their jobs every day. We are told to act small, or lean in, or speak a certain way, or dress a certain way, or climb a certain ladder, or not climb a ladder at all after having a child, or be our own boss. We go through a bunch of highs and lows and constantly deal with ever-changing work environments. If we're paying attention, we can learn from our lows. But often, we take our highs, pat ourselves on the back, and put 'em in our pockets as we move on to the next professional thing.

But at some point, in many of our careers, something freaking extraordinary happens. We accomplish something newsworthy, that has an immense impact or is a massive peak to our career. When we don't share the accomplishment widely, or our LinkedIn, TikTok, or Instagram posts don't go viral, how do others learn about what we have done? Often, if we don't have a big public platform or a C-Suite position, no one hears about these amazing things we've done. As someone who is in none of those categories (yet!), I learned that the onus is on us. We need to tell our stories and celebrate our successes!

This book is for people who are underrepresented or who feel "othered" or "less than" at a job but truly want to make a difference at work. By understanding how to navigate bumpy professional spaces and overcome self-doubt, fear, and stress, it's possible to influence others and make a meaningful difference. And do it while maintaining your sanity. There is no magic bullet or 10-step process to get you there. It is literally a journey, with many years of trial and error, failures, and successes as we learn about ourselves and build our personal and professional muscles.

This book includes real-life stories and experiences from my career journey. Each chapter ends with tips to prompt you to reflect on your own experiences. You may decide to read this book alone and apply the tips to your daily job. Or read it with a group of friends or colleagues and discuss the content over a few weeks. I hope these stories resonate and spark intriguing conversations over coffee or lunch. My journey has been a gift, and through this book, I share that gift with you. Here's how I left a legacy at my job, and the path that got me there.

This is for you.

HAVE YOU EVER WANTED to make an impact in your organization and found yourself uncertain how to approach an issue? Or were stuck juggling professional politics, or difficult colleagues? Perhaps you're an entry-level employee, new to the organization, or a middle manager with little authority. If so, this book is for you.

I won't encourage you to run through the halls of your workplace as a change evangelist or start every Zoom meeting advocating for change. I won't encourage you to hit "reply all" on emails to leadership to expand your exposure or encourage you to "speak up" in staff meetings. We're in a period in history where our culture has taught us that to make a difference we must be bold and loud, have a fierce online presence, and enter a room with confidence and gusto. This could not be further from the truth.

I'm not the loudest or smartest one in the room at work. I don't have a doctorate or an MBA. And when I left a legacy at a $100M organization, I didn't have an executive title.

Through 20 years of awesome professional successes and horrible face-plant moments, I learned how to influence others and navigate uncomfortable professional waters. If you're part of an underrepresented group in your company (perhaps you're queer, a person of color, a woman, or a man in an all-female organization), being a champion of change comes with a lot of trial, error, success, failure, and possible career risk. It can also affect your physical and mental health. Yet, it is possible to make an impact on an organization and change it for the better. Through the powers of influence, persuasion, strategy, and knowing thy self, this book will help you unlock the secrets to creating true and meaningful impact in your professional life.

You will notice Robert Cialdini's principles of influence and persuasion—Reciprocation, Commitment, Consistency, Social Proof, Authority, Liking, and

Scarcity—woven throughout various stories. I learned about these principles the "hard way" and hope that understanding their power in professional spaces helps ease and aid your enrichment.

Consider this a compilation of juicy stories and actionable lessons. You're about to read about a professional rollercoaster ride that will give you nuggets of wisdom, spark you to think about your own situation, and make you want to debrief with a friend over a glass of wine. There are times you will gasp in shock, fist pump the air, or cheer while reading these stories.

Get out a pen and paper, open the notes app on your phone, make sure you're hydrated, and get ready to absorb this. Navigating the sticky spots of professional life and influencing others is something we can all do. Take the tips in this book and put them into action today. You can do this! It doesn't matter how big or small your organization is or whether you are a new or seasoned employee. You can make a meaningful impact on your company. You can do it without an executive title....and perhaps leave a legacy while you're at it.

2

Listen, filter, thank you...next.

A FEW YEARS AGO, I mentored a college student who was an athlete at a private college on the East Coast. She was a good student who earned good grades, with a zest for life, and a go-getter attitude. After she graduated, we kept in touch as she entered the working world. She dreamed of working in the entertainment industry and was truly passionate about this career path.

I vividly remember one of our check-ins when she mentioned that she was fired from her first job. She talked about challenges with her boss and unrealistic expectations. We chatted through the details, and I chalked it up to typical young adult transition issues when leaving the academic world and joining the workforce. About six months later, she mentioned that she had been fired from her second job. With this new information, I dug a bit deeper. I asked about her behavior, the corporate dynamics, and who she spoke to about the issues at work. She mentioned that most of the advice she received, and acted on, came from her dad or social media. *Yikes*, I thought. This young 24-year-old Black woman was listening to her 60-something-year-old father for advice on how to navigate issues in an industry that he doesn't work in. This might have contributed to the issues she was having in the workplace. Yes, it may have also been her behavior or performance. But who she sought advice from was a critical piece of the puzzle.

Now, don't come for me. Definitely, there is wisdom with age, but as a former young professional woman myself, I know that navigating corporate workspaces as an entry-level employee is highly nuanced. My mentee's father told her to speak to her boss and to demand work that matched her capability and potential. This advice may have worked if she was of a different race or gender or if her tenure at the company was longer. Trusted friends and family often have our best interests in mind but might not be an appropriate fit for advice. People who are underrepresented in the workplace have to navigate conflict with a keen, strategic tact to help them reach the outcome or progress they want. "The Memo" by Minda Hart, highlights this experience expertly as she discusses the odds stacked against women of color in the workplace, coupled with career advice. It is up to you to figure out who is the best fit for advice in your workplace.

Early in my professional career, I worked for a Wall Street consulting firm—a culture that was completely foreign to me. How I got the job is still unknown because I didn't have a business background at the time. Despite being completely out of my element, every day in this fast-paced business environment I decided to "fake it till you make it." After I learned and executed my job responsibilities inside and out, I wanted to advance in the company. As an entry-level employee, I sought advice from my peers, but their advice was short-sighted and didn't help. I soon realized that I needed advice from a seasoned professional. I needed guidance from someone in a similar demographic, who was in an advanced position, and who had the influence and power to help advance my career aspirations.

My first professional mentor was a Black man in leadership at the firm. He was always busy and traveled a lot for work. After bumping into him a few times in the kitchen, I took a leap and asked him via email for a coffee chat. It took flexibility, patience with his schedule, and time to build a relationship with him. Over the next year, I learned that he was credible, trustworthy, and a great person to seek advice from. He provided insight into the business and social dynamics and truly cared about my well-being. Twenty years later, he is still someone I connect with every few years for advice and insight. Sometimes a calculated leap of faith works.

It's important that we choose the right caliber of people to let influence our professional thoughts, behaviors, and actions. Not all family members are a shoo-in for great advice. Instead, look for someone with a similar affinity or who's been where you are. They'll likely have a better understanding of unspoken nuances and give advice that can lead to a more efficient path to progress.

When I think back to my mentee and her reliance on social media for advice, I get it. These days we're all plugged into one platform or another. It's very common to open Facebook, TikTok, or Instagram and scroll for hours when we're bored, looking for advice, or in search of inspiration. The dopamine jolt we get from scrolling makes us feel good, and that makes us go back to an app over and over again. After a long day, I love a good scroll on social media while lying on the couch decompressing from my day. Yet, during these moments of mindless entertainment, we're still absorbing the information and images that we interact with.

How much influence does this information have on us? How do we measure the caliber of an individual sharing business advice on an Instagram reel, a TikTok video, or a LinkedIn post? The truth is, we can't, at least not in the seconds it takes to scroll to the next reel or post. Some may attribute credibility to the number of followers, impressive brand partnerships, or the influencer's job title, vibe, or entertainment value. But credibility in the age of quick consumable content is highly variable. In the professional space, it's easy to refer to these platforms and to listen to the advice from "successful" people on LinkedIn for their insight on how to navigate a tricky conversation or get a promotion. There is value in the exchange of this type of information. But it is truly on us to determine the credibility of the information we read, listen to, and absorb. This is something that everyone living in the 21st century regularly confronts. Who we let influence our thoughts and actions matters.

When my mentee found other women of color in her field, sought out those in leadership, and leaned on their advice, she landed a new job in entertainment. She became more selective about who she followed on social media for professional insight. Today she has used her smarts to be successful at big companies like HBO and SHOWTIME. She is *now* truly aware of the intricate dynamics of influence, credibility, and professional advice.

REFLECTION

- Who do you go to for professional advice or insight?

- Do you know who is credible and who is trustworthy in your organization?

- Review an organizational chart of your workplace. Identify two to three people that you trust and who are credible. Make a note to interact with these people more and build a relationship with them.

- How do you discern credibility online? What three characteristics does an online influencer need to have for you to listen to and/or follow their professional advice?

Who we listen to and let influence our thoughts and actions in professional life matters.

3

Stress, courage, and influence.

DID YOU KNOW THAT when you respond to a stressful situation, cortisol hormones flood your cells as you respond in a fight, flight, freeze, or fawn manner? Can you identify your go-to stress response? Mine is freeze. When stressful situations occur, I instantly freeze and try to get my brain to catch up with the physical reaction in my body and the current crazy situation that is occurring before my eyes.

Knowing your most common stress response is critical in a professional environment. You can rarely plan for stressful or difficult work situations but knowing how you typically react will help you be more effective in the moment. When stressed, are you more likely to hold back the cussing under your breath, end the conversation and make a quick exit, or tilt your head and stare at the person in confusion? Knowing yourself is key.

At a pivotal moment early in my college career, I had an experience in which my academic background spoke louder than my race. I'd just transferred from the University of Virginia (often referred to as a "public Ivy") to Rutgers University (a public university in New Jersey that did not hold the same esteem to some). My interest in public health as a major led me to meet with the undergraduate public health advisor one Tuesday afternoon in September. I knocked on her door and mentioned that I was a transfer student looking for information to become a public health major as a sophomore. She sat at her desk, blonde hair and blue eyes with a terse look on her face, looking down at her papers. She looked up at me standing outside her door and said, "We don't have enough spots. You cannot be a public health major because you missed the Intro to Public Health Class as a freshman."

I stood in the doorway of her office wondering how that could be possible. How could my desire to study public health slip away simply because I transferred in as a sophomore? Confused, I asked, "Don't you want to see my transcript?" I had to force myself to speak as I froze. At the time, I wasn't sure what I was experiencing. This woman took one look at me, my brown skin and kinky hair, and instantly told me that a major at the largest public university in New Jersey did not have room for me. I was timid, confused, and certain that she had not seen the full picture of me.

She flippantly responded, "Fine, give me your transcript." I walked into the office and handed her my transcript. Then time stood still. She looked down at my transcript and glanced back up at me about three times. Then her demeanor, tone, and energy changed instantly. She looked up at me and said slowly, "Ohh!" with a large inhale, "You went to the University of Virginia....wow...okaaaayyyy...hmm."

I stood in front of her desk, stunned at the instant transformation. She sat up straighter in her chair and said, "Well...we have this new BS/MPH program that we are piloting with six students at the university where students can earn their bachelor's and master's degrees in public health at the same time. I think you would be a good fit for that program."

My mind almost exploded! Cortisol rushed into every cell in my body. If I had fair skin, you would have seen me flushed with reaction. *Oh*, I thought, *THIS is what racism looks like. Holy cow*! It wasn't the first time I'd experienced discrimination because of my skin color, but it was definitely the first time someone did a complete 180 to my face after learning something about me on paper that challenged their idea of how I appeared.

"Um," I stuttered, "that sounds good?" shrugging my shoulders. It felt like someone had turned on a blender in my 19-year-old mind. What the heck was going on? How was I unable to be a public health major five minutes ago, and now I am being offered a spot in an elite, novel program? None of this made sense.

After that interaction, I continued my studies in public health at Rutgers University. I joined the inaugural BS/MPH class program where I received three degrees in six years (a BS and two MPH degrees). I later won a prestigious fellowship with the New Jersey Department of Health Epidemiology Program.

You are probably thinking, "Woah, this story is about straight-up racism."

Yes, it is. It is also about how one stressful encounter can alter the trajectory of your life, given you know how to respond. The power of your voice and your ability to influence others with that voice during a time of stress is unmatched. Academia is a tough place to have influence, especially in the health and medical field, where influence is typically offered to people who have terminal degrees (MD, PhD, etc.).

To have influence in academia, you often must have tenure and/or have authored a few publications to be taken "seriously." Another thing that academia accepts for influence is perceived academic prestige where the sentiment is that the closer you are to an Ivy League school, the better.

This is a highly debated concept rooted in classism, racism, and many other -isms. My attendance at the University of Virginia—the "public ivy"—influenced a woman, in the middle of her prejudiced behavior, to do an about-face. Her initial reaction and response to my race was inexcusable. Because I was familiar with my typical freeze response during stressful situations, I forced myself to speak up. This act of speaking up led her to see a fuller version of me and offer me a coveted spot in a program that catapulted my career in public health.

No one should have the power to thwart a young person's dreams based on their own biases. Yet, the reality is that Black and Brown students are often subjected to racism in academic settings. Finding the courage to navigate these situations is something students do repeatedly.

In the middle of a prejudiced act, I found courage and I spoke up. If I hadn't spoken up or hadn't pushed past my freeze response, I would have walked out of the advisor's office feeling rejected and likely chosen a different major with potentially less lucrative career opportunities. Speaking up for yourself in an uncomfortable moment allows for possibility to enter the room. Tapping into the courage to speak up is a brave act with an unpredictable outcome. For Black, Brown, and underrepresented students, it's sometimes the only option. In life, we only have control over a few things: our breath, our voice, and our reaction.

REFLECTION

- What is your common stress response? What

can you do to help yourself move past your stress response in a critical moment? Where can you draw courage from?

- Think back to when you noticed or wanted to speak up when experiencing an act of discrimination or injustice with someone else. How did it make you feel? What did you learn about yourself from it?

Self-awareness is key in uncomfortable situations. Using your voice opens the door to unpredictable outcomes that could change your life.

4

Do I like you...meh.

As a young graduate student, I won a fellowship at the Department of Health (DOH) Epidemiology Department in my home state. I was so excited when I found out that my boss was a well-published black woman with a PhD who had worked in the department for years. My epidemiology mentor was an artsy, middle-aged white man from Trenton, NJ. Both were very smart and longtime health department employees. In this fellowship, there was a requirement for my thesis to mutually benefit the graduate objectives and health department needs.

During the beginning of my two-year fellowship, I worked hard to design a mutually beneficial project. As a fellow, I spent time learning how DOH worked operationally and sat in on high-level meetings with my boss and mentor. Eager to add value, I spoke up in meetings, asked questions, and conducted myself as a typical fellow would. I was kind, polite, and respectful, however, I often had different ideas about how to approach a research angle and use newer analysis techniques. My mentor was intrigued by my input and often indulged my suggestions with a conversation, guidance, or a directive to dig a little deeper. My boss, however, did not respond the same way. She resisted my thoughts and ideas for innovation, demonstrated strong opposition, and grew to largely dislike me over time.

Over the next two years, my boss doubled down on rejecting my input at work. As a graduate fellow, this was stressful because I did all the things that I was taught in public health school. I tried dressing more professionally, getting to know her personally, speaking a certain way, not speaking up as much, and other inauthentic tactics. However, in school, I was never taught about the principle of likability. I did not learn about the nuances among women in the workplace. The strain of generational differences on a working relationship was foreign to me. I was woefully unprepared for the complicated entanglement of internalized racism and power when your boss, who shares your same gender and race, dislikes you. Issues of race, gender, and power in the workplace are intricately intertwined and require a long U.S. historical context to better understand. I would have to write another book to explain this.

Despite my efforts to get on my boss's good side, she blocked my master's thesis proposal and would not sign off on my research. My academic advisor at school signed off on my thesis proposal, but my boss did not. This was shocking and led to a steep learning curve in professional relationships. I was young, naïve, and optimistic. I didn't know how to manage the confluence of factors that were affecting my ability to succeed in this situation. Her actions could have resulted from a myriad of reasons and I didn't have the internal self-assuredness to realize that her dislike for me had less to do with me and more to do with her. But I do know that when your first black woman boss blocks your research and strongly dislikes you as a young up-and-coming black professional—it is crushing. Soul crushing. I took it very personally.

Though it was a bumpy road, I eventually finished my master's thesis, completed my fellowship, and received my graduate degree. I was unable to improve the relationship with my boss, despite my best efforts. At the end of the experience, I learned a valuable lesson. Sometimes we may not understand all the reasons behind a boss's actions or behavior, but we cannot discount likeability when trying to survive in a workplace. For women, especially women of color, it is a consequential aspect of success, like it or not.

For the next 10 years in business, I struggled to accept that likability was imperative to success at work as a woman. Deep down it was an incredibly annoying concept as I wanted to advance based on my merit and work output instead of who thought favorably of me in the office, what I wore to work, and how many social relationships I cultivated. However, the reality is that it was unavoidable.

During this time, I also learned about social capital, the hard way. For a few years at a different job, I noticed that my advancement was stunted because I didn't have any relationships with colleagues and leadership outside of the office. I was focused on doing my job during working hours and left the office as soon as I could to face my two-hour commute home. Ugh, it was a brutal commute. I soon realized that my long commute and lack of collegial relationships were holding me back. I overheard a colleague mention social capital during a lunchtime gossip session. I immediately googled it to learn more.

According to Robert Putnam, a Harvard professor who coined the term, social capital refers to the resources or capital that we gain from existing within a social network. It is a social science concept that incorporates our ability to leverage social connections, develop trust, and solve problems or take action. In a workplace setting, higher levels of social capital mean you can often achieve more, and lower levels of social capital mean it is harder to achieve the same goals.

Likability is a critical factor when building social capital. Generally, people tend to like others who are similar to them. Some individuals enjoy differences among others as that diversity inspires learning, connection, and variation. In a healthy work environment, a blend of different skills, backgrounds, and personality types forms a solid team. In environments that don't value differences, figuring out how to navigate likability to build connections is an important step, especially when you don't look, sound, or act like everyone else.

But how do we build connections when we're thrust into a new work environment with people that we don't know and may not like or trust? Connections are commonly built by getting to know a bit about someone or finding common ground with your colleagues. Research has shown that this tactic has proven to produce more mutually beneficial relationships and successful work connections. Then add gender or race to the mix, and the formula is not so cut and dry.

Specifically for women in the workplace, being likable goes beyond personality, how you treat people, skill set, or job performance. It also includes your appearance. Whether we want to admit it or not, how you look, present yourself, or wear your hair play a huge role in a woman's likability within a workplace setting. Our patriarchal society has put this in place. When female political candidates run for office, they are more likely to be judged by public opinion on their appearance, their pantsuit, wrinkles, or grey hair, as opposed to their platform, voting history, or ability to lead as a public servant.

Likeability for women in the workplace is an inescapable requirement to get things done. Now add sexuality, race, or ableism to the mix. When one's identity has multiple layers (e.g. Latino, queer, disabled) an employee's experience with likability is highly nuanced and complex. Their experience may be filled with assumptions, microaggressions, and preconceived notions on both sides. Thus, making it even more difficult to navigate likability and make connections with colleagues.

At the end of the day, whether we like it or not, likability and social capital are here to stay. As a young graduate student, I followed guidance from professional development books that focused on getting the job done, presenting a good image, building relationships with your colleagues, impressing your boss, etc. All these factors are important when entering a new environment or for a young employee entering the workforce. I tried all these tactics. However, likability is one of the most critical factors in getting things done, building collegial relationships, and stocking up on social capital in a work environment.

Now, I invest in social capital from the moment I start a new job. I have found success by observing the company culture, understanding colleagues' motivations, acting strategically, developing my own measure of success, and engaging with others in an authentic way that fits my level of comfort. That last part is tough. The traditional wisdom to "just be yourself" is poor advice, in my opinion. Some call it selective authenticity. Sometimes we need to bring different parts of ourselves to our jobs every day. And quite honestly, some parts of ourselves should stay at home. You know which ones I'm talking about. Since we're all multilayered, multifaceted people, we must create our personal definition of authenticity and then decide how and when to activate our authentic selves.

This journey has taught me that personal growth is incredibly important as a professional. The peaks and valleys of navigating social capital and likeability in my career were rough. So rough, it would require a large bottle of red wine to share all the stories. But I am grateful for that initial experience as a graduate fellow.

It opened a door for me to understand the immense value of a few principles that I brushed off as unimportant. Silly me. I hope this accelerates your awareness, acceptance, and action on this front.

REFLECTION

- Have you observed what traits or behaviors make people likable in your workplace?

- Write down all the things you like about yourself. Which ones do you want to focus on others liking about you?

- Have you invested in social capital in your workplace? If not, what can you do to start prioritizing professional connections tomorrow?

- What have been the benefits and challenges of using strategic authenticity in your workplace?

In a new business environment, you must invest in social capital and likability in ways that are the most authentic for you.

5

Hold your cards close or play your hand.

ONE YEAR, AS A new employee at a company, I went through a season of mental gymnastics where I psychoanalyzed, hemmed, hawed, and had many happy hour drinks with friends to try to figure out how to advance on my team. I wanted to set myself up for a senior role in middle management. I knew that I was hired based on my interviews, work experience, and, quite possibly, likeability. But, I also knew that I had skills outside of my job function that were not on my resume or LinkedIn profile. I had a host of unique skills and uncommon perspectives that could add value to my team and my company.

Regularly, I would lay in bed before going to sleep trying to figure out the benefits, consequences, or opportunities to share more of myself at work. I know this sounds a little heady, but as a recovering type-A individual, I wanted to do my very best and succeed at this company. For example, if I shared with everyone that I was a yoga teacher, would I then be the resident yogi and asked to hold corporate yoga sessions? Would I be considered a soft peacemaker and not be taken seriously as a strong negotiator by leadership? Or do I tell everyone on my team that my background in statistics means that I can evaluate programs and determine ROI quickly and effectively without trying very hard—even though I was not hired in the data or business department?

 I grappled with the question of when, how, and with whom I should share this information. I went in mental circles trying to figure out whether I should put all my skills on the table for my boss and colleagues or hold some back and strategically share when an opportunity arose. This may seem like a trivial thing to obsess about. But in the past, I'd received advice that encouraged me to just share my skills. A prior colleague said, "Go ahead, put them out there so you can hit the ground running and demonstrate your complete value-add up front." And I followed this advice.

As an eager bright-eyed new employee, I shared all my skills, tricks, and ideas upfront. I was eager to impress my superiors. However, this approach often did not work in my favor. It typically prompted additional work classified as "stretch projects" that were not necessarily tied to a raise or title upgrade. For some, it might work in their favor and lead to a salary increase or advanced positioning on their team. But for me, I always had to work hard and hope all angles aligned for a promotion. It never came easy to me. That's when I learned about the principle of scarcity from a few MBA friends. It helped me advance through the ranks of my company more quickly and thoughtfully.

We've all experienced the concept of scarcity when booking a hotel room. Have you ever searched for a hotel room and seen *Book now – only 2 rooms left at your rate* on the screen? What did you do after reading this? Initially, it made me hurry up and decide if I wanted to stay at this hotel or book another one quickly. After a while, I realized that some sites use this to encourage the customer to make the sale. This is a marketing technique that squarely leans on the persuasion principle of scarcity. According to Robert Caldini, the principle of scarcity states that rare or unique objects, ideas, and information hold greater value than a more common version. When used to influence and persuade, you will notice scarcity at play where information or an object is in short supply, in high demand, or only available for a limited time. In the workplace, scarcity can be used to convince others to take our advice, buy into our suggestions, or support our business proposals.

When I learned about this principle, I became more thoughtful about how and when I shared the skills or insights that were outside of the scope of my daily job function. I learned to strategically use the principle of scarcity to find an opportune time to share my unique skill or perspective. If I had something to add on a team call that could propel the team or solve a problem, I taught myself to pause in the moment, think about the best way to share the information, and then share it strategically (whether it be in the moment, in an email, on the next call, or to my boss in person). I practiced this repeatedly in the workplace.

Eventually, using this principle helped me differentiate myself from my team and create a sense of added value during a time of need. Adopting strategic sharing and documenting my input in writing (i.e., via a follow-up email), allowed me to ensure that my ideas were attributed to my brain trust and limited the ability of someone else to take credit for my novel ideas.

One day on a hike, a good friend shared how scarcity can be used with work products as well. She previously worked for a large corporate company in the HR department. Her team was responsible for leadership training that was available to all employees year-round. The training was poorly attended and didn't produce the results that the HR team desired. Her team first improved the content and instruction within the training. After a soft launch, the number of training participants still did not increase. The entire team was disappointed and quickly began to search for new solutions. During a brainstorming session, one team member suggested changing the structure of the offering to increase interest and buy-in. The following year, the team changed the entire offering structure. They made the inclusion criteria more selective and participation by invitation only. The training schedule was changed from a year-round offering to only twice a year. It was marketed as a unique training opportunity that was only available for a limited time, to a select few. After launching the new training format and inclusion criteria, the participation numbers increased dramatically. The value of the training exponentially increased due to integrating the principle of scarcity that increased buy-in and demand as a unique opportunity.

Keep in mind that my friend and her team needed access to a level of power and authority to change the offering structure of the training at a large company. The team also took on a level of risk, which is always present when changing or modifying something. Making the training more scarce was a risk that turned out well for this team. The principle of scarcity worked in their favor.

Whether it's transforming a product or deciding how you want to position yourself within the company or team to demonstrate your value, there's a fine line between risks and benefits. It is all a matter of strategy. Be strategic about when, how, and with whom you decide to share your unique skills, talents, and perspectives in the workplace. Be clear about what you want to get out of the interaction of sharing. Put on your strategy glasses to determine the best course of action. Your unique insights, tips, and skills are important. They are your personal intellectual property! Treat them as such. Strategy mixed with a persuasion technique, like scarcity, can help cement your value in a company.

REFLECTION

- When have you seen the principle of scarcity used in your workplace?

- What skills, ideas, or perspectives (outside of your job function) do you have that might add value to your team? When do you plan to share them?

Scarcity can transform how you position yourself as an asset to your company.

6

Influence by the worker bee.

DID YOU KNOW THAT worker bees are the backbone of a beehive? They are the only ones to produce beeswax and make honey. They gather nectar from flowers and bring it back to the hive to turn it into honey. The queen and the drone bees never make honey. When you are in a worker bee role in an organization, your job largely relies on executing the tasks given to you by your boss. You are typically hired for your expertise and then tasked to execute someone else's vision. Some workplaces have a truly collaborative approach while others are more hierarchical in their approach.

Sometimes as a worker bee, we have the opportunity to influence our programs or projects and create impressive products for our organizations. But how often do we get to be the megaphone that amplifies the positive transformation, and receive due credit for our work? As a worker bee, the opportunity to share our work product typically relies on our manager or the hierarchies within the organization. Or perhaps, it could also rely on us.

Early in my career, I worked at a hospital with a residency program in social medicine in New York City. Social medicine is a concept that seeks to improve health through clinical care, community outreach, research, and advocacy. This residency program trained new physicians to work with underserved populations, empowering them to be a vehicle for social change. As the only master's level employee in the department, I was tasked with many projects, including running a government grant with seven micro-projects, educating physicians on Public Health 101, and integrating continuous improvement into education mechanisms.

Halfway through my tenure, I was asked to revise the department's signature, month-long course "Intro to Social Medicine" for first-year residents. I built a team consisting of an EdD, two MDs, and two PhDs. Together, we assessed the course, worked with other staff, and integrated aspects of experiential learning into the program. Under the new curriculum, residents not only learned the core tenets of social medicine but also visited Rikers Island, one of the most notorious jails in America, to learn about recidivism and health care. We also spent time at local botánicas to learn about the cultural medical practices of some Latino and Hispanic patients. The curriculum was a dynamic success and resulted in a peer-reviewed journal publication. We submitted an abstract to present our work at a medical education conference in Cuba and were accepted. Then came the task of deciding who should attend the conference.

In the healthcare space, traditional and outdated value systems align the perception of expertise with a few factors: first, possession of a terminal degree (MD or PhD); second, significant publication in a highly reputable, peer-reviewed journal; third, tenure or a professorship at an academic institution; and fourth, leadership of a healthcare organization. Given academia's preference for expertise aligned with terminal degrees, I knew that as the only master's level person on the team and the department worker bee, I would be last on the list. But I led the entire project and conducted

80% of the work. Two of the M.D.s and the Ed.D. were in favor of my attendance. However, the dean of the department had never sent a staff member (i.e., a worker bee) on an international trip with department funding.

Eager to go to Cuba and present my work, I petitioned the dean. My supervisor advised me to write a formal letter explaining why I should attend. I followed that with an in-person appeal to highlight my work on the project and the value-add of my attendance for the department. After a few weeks, I was granted the green light to attend the conference, fully paid. I was ecstatic! I successfully advocated up the chain, through the forest of higher-ups, and onto an international stage in Cuba. I demonstrated that a worker bee could produce great work, is worthy of department-level travel support, and can successfully represent the institution on an international platform.

Why did the dean say yes? Why do people ever say yes? The persuasion principle of reciprocation asserts that there is an inherent human attitude to try to repay, in kind, what another person has provided you. As a worker bee, I invoked the power of reciprocation and persuaded the dean to support my attendance at the conference based on my contributions and value to the department. Though we rarely get a chance to know why someone says yes, principles like reciprocation and trustworthiness are important factors that contribute to one person's ability to persuade another.

Traveling to Cuba was an amazing, life-changing experience rich with culture, history, and connection, and it was my first successful presentation on an international stage. Remember, worker bees are the only bees that make honey, and honey is treasured throughout the entire world. Promote and share the value that your honey adds, so others know how great you are!

REFLECTION

- Can you highlight an example in your professional life where the principle of reciprocation was involved in someone saying "yes" to your request? How did it make you feel? Were you courageous, brave, or scared when presenting your offer?

- How can you tactfully lean on reciprocation

in your current work environment to influence change?

48

When you get the chance to shoot your shot, take it. You can shine your light when others may not be able to see it.

7

When to walk away fast, or maybe run!

THERE IS A VIRAL video on TikTok of Deepak Chopra's voice stating, "When you have a bad day, give up. Go home and sleep. Screw it. Try again tomorrow. Not every bad day can become a good day...Go home. Save your energy. Tomorrow is another day." If only we could go to sleep in the middle of the workday when we're having a bad day. Wouldn't that be amazing! But in every bad moment, we're faced with the internal question: When should I throw in the towel, when should I quit, and how much crazy can I or should I handle? Resilience is a tricky concept in the workplace. When people truly care about an organization, project, or mission, they will demonstrate an otherworldly level of resilience, despite walking through mud every day with bare feet. But a determined spirit to make a difference may not always be worth it.

When entering a new work environment, it's sometimes easy to see the flaws, issues, and blind spots in a company upfront. Other times, issues are revealed like a slow burn as you learn the ins and outs of the company. Typically, when you start a new job, you are granted a period of onboarding time to learn about the company, the employees, and the policies. However, with every new company, there is a second layer of lessons to be learned. The personalities, politics, and power dynamics are the critical layer that provides insight into how things really get done. It's important to test the waters and see how things operate before you decide if you want to influence change, and whether it will be worth your energy, time, and mental health.

About six years into my career, I got a job at a private company on the East Coast. Before that job, I primarily worked for healthcare organizations where the essence of altruism was directly or indirectly palpable. In this new arena, the atmosphere was full of a spirit to make the client happy and bring in money for the firm.

Although I had some experience in the business world, I was still learning the importance of understanding power dynamics and playing "office politics." The office politics game looks different at each company. At this firm, it included showing my face at company events, water cooler banter, pretending I loved my job, and liaising with colleagues outside of the office for drinks even though I had a long commute home. During my first seven months, I observed the dynamics of the company led by two white men who were savvy businesspeople. I quickly noticed that they got away with saying absurd things to employees without repercussion. It was a fast-growing company with a disempowered HR director and a very unclear path of ethics.

Within a year, I watched my boss stealthily maneuver and manipulate her way up the management chain. Although she was a staunch advocate for female leadership and development, her business tactics outside of my mostly female team were suspect. If I had a crystal ball and someone told me that her tactics would promote her to executive leadership within the decade, I would have approached many situations differently.

The work environment was toxic, and I had been assigned a challenging project rife with problems that no one in the company wanted to work on. A client on this project was a friend of the company president, so leadership was invested in my ability to fix the issues in the project. Then my direct boss went on maternity leave and I was left in charge of our woman-dominated team. For the next four months, I was to report directly to a new vice president who was brought in especially to handle important projects. My new boss was a misogynistic white man in his late 40s with an ego the size of Texas.

Mr. Texas Ego was extremely condescending, pompous, and always right with a smile. He had a lot of influence in the company. He consistently tried to coach me on my difficult project but most of his advice came from a place of privileged, white male superiority, and ego—all of which were largely unhelpful to a rising black woman professional. I did not know how to adapt my voice to this new business setting with a new boss. How was I supposed to talk, elevate, or provide constructive feedback in an environment that was so foreign? Imposter syndrome was in full effect as I tried to do everything right. I constantly worried about messing up, receiving disapproval from my new boss, or upsetting a client. I made myself small every day while running a multi-million-dollar account. This overarching fear stifled me and stagnated my progress in the firm. I witnessed other colleagues rise through the ranks, get promotions, and travel the world, while I was stuck on a seemingly impossible project tasked to ameliorate all its problems.

In true optimist fashion, I took on the challenge and truly believed that I could change the trajectory of this holistically crappy work situation. I went about working the best way I could. I cozied up to our client. I learned how to speak corporate. I worked and worked and worked. I mentored and managed the women employees on my team and held the entire account together while my boss was on maternity leave. I put in long hours and many evenings consisted of a bottle of Two Buck Chuck wine, a microwave meal, and my computer. I was constantly trying to please everyone at work—my boss, the client, and the president (who was personally invested in my project). My own mental health and physical well-being were in serious decline, and I was taking horrible care of myself.

Here's the ugly truth: It worked! After a few months, I was rocking and rolling on the project and in my professional life. Things were going well, and I successfully figured out how to navigate the rocky ship with grace and multiple client successes. My health was in fast decline, but I did not care. I was excelling at work. During our review, Mr. Texas Ego took me into his office and congratulated me on my success. He ended the conversation by saying, "I'm so glad I fixed you," and giving me a huge toothy grin.

Stunned and taken aback, I said nothing. Literally, nothing. (There goes that freeze stress response again.) I sat there with the stone-cold, unemotional face that I'd learned in corporate America. *Did this man really congratulate himself for fixing me?* I wondered. *WTF?*

He later gave me a $20,000 raise and a corresponding promotion. Thankful, but confused and mad, I was stuck. I did not report him. I did not talk to HR. I just took the promotion and swallowed my rage. Talk about an insane situation. Crappy mental health, work success, a horrible, misogynistic boss, and a $20,000 raise. In true city-girl fashion, I celebrated with my girlfriends by simultaneously venting and rejoicing at a rooftop bar brunch in Manhattan.

When my boss came back from maternity leave, she thanked me for holding the team together and we continued business as usual. A few months later, there was a major issue with my client. Someone within the partnership did not show up for a high-profile speaking event in Chicago. The next morning, I was summoned into a meeting with the president and my boss. The president proceeded to berate me for 30 minutes, yelling at me at the top of his lungs, and blaming me for the unexpected actions of a grown man in Chicago.

Imagine receiving a loud, verbal reprimand in a newsroom-style office where the glass wall in his office shook due to his yelling. My boss, that staunch advocate of female empowerment, sat there and watched him yell at me. She said nothing and remained quiet. She did not stick up for me or support me in any way. I walked out of that room, hysterical and in tears, and went straight to HR. The disempowered HR director gave the president a slap on the wrist, and I received an inauthentic, half-spirited apology. Trust in my boss went completely out the window as she had played politics for her self-preservation and fed me to the wolves.

What would you have done in this situation? My stubborn persistence took over and I was determined to turn things around. But a month and a half later, I learned that one of the partners on my project had mismanaged funding. I had the records, the details, and the "receipts" as they say. I informed my boss, who sent the issue up to the president of the company. I documented the information, spoke honestly, and tried to uphold my values of transparency and integrity. After a few weeks of communication, ultimately no action was taken by the company or the partners. All parties were willing to ignore the issue. Continuing to manage this partnership and this account was against my core value of integrity as a leader. I could not be a transparent leader knowing that fiscal accountability was not enforced. Verbal abuse, manipulative leadership tactics, unethical fiscal actions, no accountability, and an overall toxic environment led me to resign from the company. Sometimes when you have a bad day, or multiple bad days that span many months, it's time to give up. Go home and sleep, as Deepak Chopra advises.

I genuinely wanted to influence change in some way, but the environment itself was unchangeable and some of my colleagues were not going anywhere. Many times we work in inflexible and unhealthy environments. You may find that the personalities, politics, and power dynamics are outside of your realm of control or influence. Self-awareness is crucial when you analyze the dynamics of a toxic work environment. Separate yourself from the situation and spend time reflecting. Wise friends Arianne Graham and Dr. Sara Woodruff once gave me the five commandments of working in a toxic work environment.

Remember these commandments the next time you find yourself in a crappy work environment:

1. It's likely that you are not depressed; you are just disappointed.

2. You alone cannot cure this f*ckery. So, stop trying.

3. Remember that hurt people hurt people.

4. Don't get distracted. Make sure you are working

towards the bullet points you want on your resume.

5. Know when to get out.

Sometimes knowing when to get the heck out is the best course of action. It is a common struggle. I did not find my voice; I did not speak up or out. I quit and found a great therapist FAST.

REFLECTION

- Have you ever worked in a toxic work environment?

- How did you navigate that environment? What were the effects on your physical and emotional health?

- In what areas do you need to trust yourself, your gut, or your intuition at work? What can you do to find distance from the issue and spend time tapping inward to listen to yourself?

Sometimes a desire to be a great employee cannot supersede the personalities, politics, and power dynamics in a toxic environment. Make the right decision for your mental and emotional health.

Always look back.

SOMETIMES WE HAVE INFLUENCE over our organizations and yet do not get to reap the benefits of our labor while we're working at the company. Everyone is familiar with the exit interview where you go balls to the wall giving insight and feedback and telling the HR representative what you *really* think about your manager or that team member who threw you under the bus. One may hope that in those instances, the HR person takes the gems out of your exit interview and passes them on. However, we don't usually know what happens to the insight we share.

Often, it's taken with a grain of salt, and the HR representative and the company move on with life after you leave. Or the opposite happens, and you learn that after you leave, leadership listened and implemented your idea but chose your departure to be their catalyst for change. Oh, these instances are the most frustrating!

But I learned that when this happens, it is very important to look back. What you find might be helpful to add to your resume as a success story or a professional achievement. A clean slate is important as you move on to your next venture, but don't forget to look back. Talk to an old colleague, find out if they implemented any of your ideas, and make sure to put that on your resume. That is the product of your influence. We are not responsible for understanding the reasons why folks choose to change or shift, but it is important that we take our flowers when they are due to us because we planted the seeds.

At one point in my career, I worked on a team of educators and trainers for patients and advocates with rare diseases. At one training session, I met a patient advocate who was a middle-aged white woman from New Hampshire. During the training, she came up to me and asked, "You look like, you know who?"

"Who?" I asked, curious to hear her answer as I was often a doppelganger for many people.

"You know, you look like that colored girl," she said, nodding her head and giving me a light tap on the shoulder.

Did she seriously just call me *colored*? My brain was flooded with shock, disbelief, and confusion. I froze and tried to compose myself while confronting a racial slur.

"You know," she continued. "You look like the woman with the hair."

My face scrunched up.

"You know that woman who does movies with the braids."

At this point, I had a million thoughts and emotions. "Do you mean Ava Duverney?"

"Yeah, that's her!" she said. Her demeanor was cheery and upbeat. She spoke as though she just paid me a compliment, completely unaware that she had just used a racial slur to my face.

I immediately walked away, contemplating how to best deal with this situation at my new job. By that point in my life, I had learned the art of non-reaction, which underrepresented people sometimes adopt in settings where they are not in the majority. In this instance of stress and shock, my response was not fight or flight, but rather freeze and stare at this woman like she had three heads.

Instead of confronting the woman directly, I raised the issue later on with my manager during our next one-on-one meeting. She was shocked and implied that she would do something about it. Six months went by, and she did nothing about it. The issue was pushed under the rug until we had a meeting to discuss our difficult working dynamic which was heavily tainted by her inaction from my racist encounter. Given that she was the mother of biracial children, I naïvely expected her to do something about the situation. This was my first mistake. I was reminded of my first lesson in professional life. If you don't advocate for yourself, no one will. You cannot leave it up to someone else to advocate on your behalf, even if they say they will.

During our discussion, I mentioned the need for DEI (diversity, equity, inclusion) sessions and integration into our work. I also suggested health equity integration into the overall work of this health-related non-profit. True to form, she tasked me with doing presentations on those topics for staff, state chapters, and patients. I agreed and continued to educate the entire organization on these principles. During that time, I kept enforcing the need to hire someone to do the health equity and/or DEI work for the company. I even wrote a grant and brought in the first health equity funding for the organization totaling over a quarter million dollars.

Taking on the unpaid burden of organizational transformation is something people of color have been asked to do for decades when it comes to DEI and similar subject matter areas. For this reason and others, I subsequently resigned from the organization. Before I left, I spoke to the CEO about my thoughts and suggestions for DEI and health equity integration and operations. I gave insight on how to develop a strategy and actions that would go beyond a public statement.

Five months after I left the job, I received an email from my previous boss saying that they had created a Vice President of Health Equity position and wanted me to apply for it. They also invested in DEI consultants to work with leadership on issues of inequity at the organization.

I was already on to my next job but was both pleased and frustrated that they took my advice after I left. That, however, did not stop me from including this professional win on my resume. I influenced this organization to create an operational and financial commitment to health equity and DEI advancement. Even though I was out the door, with no desire to look back, I did anyway. I looked back, celebrated my win, and moved on with my life.

And if you are wondering, I did not take the job. No way, but my win is a bright, shiny bullet on my resume.

You may never know whether you made an impact on an organization if you don't look back. Find an avenue of information, look back briefly, see if there are any fruits from your tenure, and continue moving forward. Do this in the healthiest and best way for yourself. It could be in the form of an email, a quick phone chat, a social media inquiry to a colleague, coffee with an old colleague, or just the rumor mill. After you briefly look back, take stock of anything valuable and proceed toward the next season in your life. Remember, you can look backward while still moving forward.

REFLECTION

- How often have you looked back at a prior organization to see if the breadcrumbs you left were swept under the rug or made into a delicious meal?

- Depending on your reason for leaving, how can you reconnect and poke around to see if your boss, supervisor, or colleagues took your suggestions while employed?

Look back, get your flowers, and put them on your resume while moving forward.

9

When personal and professional worlds collide.

Have you ever started a job intending to do one thing and ended up doing something completely different? Sometimes our intentions in life produce different results than what we originally envisioned or imagined. When this happens, it's important to stay open to the possibilities and be present to what is happening around you.

In the middle of the COVID-19 pandemic, I took a job at the largest maternal and child health advocacy and research organization in the United States. This was a well-known non-profit with over 600 employees. I was tasked with creating the Health Equity department, transforming its health equity practices, and integrating principles into key touch points within the organization. I was well-suited for this job given my background in health disparities and organizational transformation.

This new position came at a time when many organizations increased their commitment to equity and diversity after the murder of George Floyd and the racial reckoning in the summer of 2020. During this time the entire world was confronting a deadly global pandemic, layered on top of a racial awakening within the U.S.

Though well-intentioned, many companies during that time hired equity professionals but provided them with sparse resources, little authority, and no internal support. In this role, I had a large task and very few human or financial resources to adequately execute the job. Despite this, I thoroughly enjoyed the job as it allowed space for me to lead, educate, advise, and act as a vehicle of change. Add to that the fact that I truly believed in the vision of the organization and I was all in.

At this large organization with over 30 local regions, I spent a lot of time speaking, educating, and providing strategic insight on maternal and child health equity issues. Nothing was easy. It took time, persistence, and dedication to get anything done. As I built relationships over Zoom, I learned about the social fabric of the organization, the power dynamics, and the true intentions and underlying motives of my colleagues.

Thankfully, at this point in my career, I'd come across a whole host of characters in various organizations with similar archetypes. For example, the climber who is dead set on getting ahead, the lifer who is a master at office politics chess, the underutilized colleague, the overworked one who loves being a martyr, the kind-hearted, smart colleague who is always taken for granted, the power-hungry new hire, the senior leader that holds all the power, and many more.

As the underutilized colleague, I deeply understood the unspoken dynamics of the organizational environment. Every day felt like a whirlwind of new assignments, fires to put out, educating colleagues, consulting on corporate proposals, advising teams, leading projects outside of my scope, filling in for higher-ups, and strategy meetings to maximize the impact of this $100M non-profit. Despite the chaos, I enjoyed working with my colleagues to make a difference in the communities we served.

Two years into my time at the job, my husband and I were expecting our first child. As a pregnant woman over 40, the beginning of my pregnancy was routine but with the typical precautions of someone in my situation. I continued to work, teach yoga, and enjoy my new pregnancy bliss. After a while, pregnancy complications landed me in the hospital.

My doctor was not on call the night that I was admitted, but she sent another doctor friend to check on me. I remember laying in the hospital bed in the labor and delivery room, hooked up to machines and medicine when Dr. C. walked into the room at 2 a.m. We chatted for about 10 minutes. She comforted my fears and assured me that I was in the best hospital and had a great team working on my behalf. She also mentioned that her daughter was born three months early, about 20 years ago, and is now heading to college. This was encouraging.

During that conversation, she mentioned having to go back to work two weeks after delivery because she had to save her maternity leave for when her daughter came home from the Neonatal Intensive Care Unit (NICU). Immediately I thought: *Wow! I can't believe she had to do that. I have no idea how she managed to work in a hospital for two months while her baby was in the NICU upstairs. All while she was still recovering from delivery. We were so backward 20 years ago. Thank God we have progressed.*

Little did I know, this thought would come to haunt me.

***

I spent one month in the hospital and delivered my son prematurely close to the Christmas holiday. He was expected to spend the next three months in the NICU. Exhausted from the emergency C-section and a flood of postpartum hormones, I managed to notify my company's HR contact that I had delivered and would be using my paid family leave effective immediately.

Before this phone call, I knew that I had 12 weeks of paid family leave and planned to couple that with sick leave and vacation time. Though I worked for the largest U.S. non-profit focused on maternal and child health, I knew that in a country with no universal paid family leave as of 2021, the 12 paid weeks that they offered was light years ahead of some U.S. companies who offer one to two weeks for mothers and often no paid time for partners. And yet, they were still eons behind many developed nations that offer workers six to 12 months of parental leave.

Still, none of these calculations included a contingency if your baby needed an extended hospital stay in the NICU or was born with special needs. All mothers and parents, regardless of the outcome of their birth and the health of their child, were given the same amount of paid family leave.

As I lay on my bed healing from major surgery, on the phone with the HR person, the realization slowly came to me like a freight train coming to a slow stop at a station. The wheels screeched, and I could smell the burning iron as the air was filled with soot and smoke.

Wait, I thought. *If I'm only given 12 weeks of paid leave, and my son will be in the hospital for about 12 weeks due to prematurity...what am I going to do when he comes home from the hospital? If I use up all of my family leave while he is in the hospital, I will only have a few saved vacation days to spend with him when he comes home. I will have to return to work before establishing a breastfeeding routine, bonding with him, and figuring out our new family rhythm.*

Honestly, time slowed down during that moment and the birth of this realization was as painful as labor pains. *No, no, no...* I thought in a panic. *This can't be right.*

That night, I scoured through the employee handbook over and over again. I read the lines under paid family leave eight times to make sure I did not miss anything in my hormonal fog. But no. I had read it right. There were no contingencies for families that had babies in the NICU.

Mind you, I worked for the largest maternal and child health advocacy organization in the country. NICU education was a cornerstone of their services. Still, they gave all employees the same amount of paid leave, regardless of their pregnancy outcome.

Quickly, my shock turned into anger as I cried and cried and cried to my husband for the next few days. How in the world do they expect us all to recover *and* spend time with our babies if I, like many others, have sick babies who need more care and medical attention?

The amount of rage, anger, disappointment, and help-lessness I felt could have filled three Olympic-sized swimming pools.

The next few days were a blur as I tried to figure out how to navigate this new reality. The Facebook blogs and online groups mentioned that this was an ongoing and undercover problem that many women just grin and bear. When you have a newborn baby in the NICU, the entire family—especially the mother—is in crisis mode.

Each day we drove to the hospital where my husband pushed me in a wheelchair up to the NICU to see our newborn baby. We talked to doctors, conferred with the nurses, and prayed constantly for his con-tinued growth and development. The physical pain of the abdominal sutures from my C-section was intense but nothing compared to the emotional pain of those weeks. When I say this was torture, it was pure, raw, stripped-down, vulnerable torture of a mother's mind, body, and spirit.

Yet at the same time, I needed to deal with my job.

Somehow, during moments of clarity, recovery, and pumping breast milk every three hours (through the night) for my baby in the hospital—my professional brain kicked in. I figured out a way to project manage my way through this situation. I read blogs and saw TikTok posts that many women went back to work early to save their leave so that they could spend time with their babies when they got out of the hospital. Just like Dr. C., who I met in the labor and delivery unit the night I was admitted to the hospital. I could not believe that I had to face the same issue that a doctor 20 years older than me dealt with 20 years ago. I was outraged, to say the least.

When I regained my composure, I created a spreadsheet. I came to the conclusion that I would return to work six weeks after the birth, work for about six weeks, then go back on maternity leave for six weeks and tack on some personal vacation time and unpaid time off. This plan would allow me to spend time with my newborn when he came home from the NICU.

My obstetrician signed off on the plan and mentioned that many of her patients had to do the same thing. I got on the phone again with HR to explain my plan. They were amenable to it and admitted that no one had ever done this before.

I could not imagine that in an organization with 600+ employees, zero families had a NICU stay and returned to work early, needing to save their paid family leave. It was statistically impossible for my family to be the first to go through this in a 75-year-old organization. What likely happened is that employees did not disclose their situation and, instead, pushed through a tough situation. Or they left the organization after their paid leave was complete. Oftentimes faceless and voiceless employees remain that way until someone decides to pay attention to them. I wrestled with the gaping blind spot in this organization and, likely, within others.

A little over a month after delivering my baby, I logged back on to my work computer and went back into the full-time working world. Even though I passed my six-week post-delivery checkup, I had a host of postpartum problems that I faced quietly while on work calls and conducting everyday business. Many of my colleagues were confused as to why I was back at work so quickly. Most were shocked when I explained my need to save paid family leave, especially given the nature of the organization.

Each day, I woke up after pumping breast milk every three hours through the night, drove to the hospital to see my baby and talk to doctors, and then logged on to my computer. Sometimes I logged in from the hospital to participate in work calls and conduct business from 1 p.m. to 7 p.m. This was my every day for a month and a half. You're probably wondering why I didn't stop working. Many new parents with babies in the NICU in the U.S. must return to work because they can't afford not to. With an anticipated three-month hospital stay, we expected a $500,000 hospital bill and had to navigate that through insurance and our salaries. For families in the U.S. who have sick newborns, not returning to work is rarely an option.

How does a person adequately perform at work while they are juggling a personal crisis? Do you create boundaries? Do you push through? Do you ask for help? Do you get another job? These are just some of the gut-wrenching questions that people in personal crises ask themselves.

For my family, we pushed through it. My husband and I were grateful to have understanding supervisors who allowed us to alter our work schedules and work from home. This is a privilege that many are not afforded, like Dr. C. who had to return to work two weeks after giving birth. Though we had support, my professional and personal relationships were strained during this time. Nothing can prepare you for the stress of having a hospitalized newborn, your body recovering from surgery, and going to work each day. No past professional experience prepared me for this reality and I found very little on the internet about "how to make this season work." Many employees in this situation are in over their heads and are literally just trying to survive while holding on to their entire family, trying to keep everyone afloat, and not drowning themselves.

Emotionally, I was a wreck. I resented moms who had full-term, easy pregnancies and deliveries. I worried about my baby's health every single hour. I was outraged that NICU families were short changed when it came to family leave, and heartbroken that so many families were facing these struggles in silence. And through it all, I prayed my own health wouldn't collapse further under the weight of the stress. It was exhausting. Every day during those six weeks, I ran on empty, just trying to survive.

One day while driving home from the NICU, I was on the phone when a work colleague told me that the company president asked about my whereabouts in a meeting. I realized from this comment that very few people knew about my situation. Remote work allows us to only show colleagues our "Zoom Face" without insight into what is happening in our personal lives. This was a challenge, along with maintaining work and life boundaries while working professionally on the same issues I was facing each day. What do you do when your personal and professional lives collide? It would be similar to having cancer, undergoing chemotherapy, and working at a cancer institution all at the same time. People do it. But the parallels, blurred lines, triggers, and attempts to cope in real-time can be overwhelming. However, when I heard that the president asked about my whereabouts, I knew that I had to send out an email explaining my situation.

I knew that I wanted to accomplish a few things in the email: One, share that I delivered my baby early and that he was in the hospital; two, tell leadership about my new work schedule—NICU in the morning and work in the afternoon; and three, tell them about other organizations that offer options for parents like me. Through my research, I learned of organizations and countries that offer NICU-specific leave and extra time for parents who have babies that need extended hospital stays. However, when I sat down to write this email, all the anger and annoyance that I had inside me came out in semi-professional word vomit. This has happened to all of us occasionally. You know, when you are trying to express yourself but are either still angry about a situation or are still processing and it comes out like mush. Here is the first draft of that mush:

Hi Everyone,

Many of you have asked for an update so I thought I would send a quick email. My son was born in December. Even though he was born prematurely, he is doing well in the NICU. He is growing and passing his preemie milestones day by day. Many of the challenges that we discuss related to Black Maternal Health happened to me. Despite access to all the resources, knowledge, and prevention mechanisms—the statistics hold true. All in all, I'm grateful that we are okay as we navigate new waters as NICU parents and the postpartum peri-od. Why am I back at work so soon:

- *Similar to many NICU moms around the country, I am splitting my maternity leave (or saving the bulk of it) so that I can spend time with my son when he comes home from the NICU.*

  - *I took some time to recover from the delivery - I am currently returning to work for a few months - then I will be back on leave when he comes home from the NICU (hopefully in March).*

  - *Our organization offers many buckets of leave to utilize outside of paternity leave (i. e. PTO, Sick, and Short-Term Disability) — however no one "plans" to have a preterm birth and most moms with children in the intensive care unit want to save options for when their child comes home. Navigating life after the NICU with a preemie can present its own set of new pathways. Many parents have had to do the same thing.*

- *A few weeks ago, a TikTok went viral on this*

topic. Many news articles picked it up:

- *https://www.today.com/parents/moms/mom -shares-tiktok-returning-work-12-days birth-rcna13075*

- *NICU Mom Shares Sad TikTok About Maternity Leave - Motherly*

• *An example of a company that offers dedicated paid leave for NICU families (in addition to family leave).*

- *"This is one of the first companies we've heard of to provide dedicated leave to support NICU families. Keeping parents and NICU babies together during a hospital stay is critical to ensure the best possible outcomes for these families." —Keira Sorrells, Preemie Mom, Founder & Executive Director NICU Parent Network*

- *https://newsroom.pinterest.com/en/post/pint erest-introduces-new-andextended-parent al-benefits-for-employees*

Often those who bring attention to an issue do not get to experience the benefits of change or transformation if they occur. Despite this, I hope this info spreads aware-ness for potential internal and external advocacy op-portunities. Please feel free to pass this on to whoever may benefit from the update or information.

I am so grateful for your support during this time!

Warmest Regards, Sherenne

After I wrote the first draft of mush, I knew that it needed a second set of eyes. I wanted this email to potentially reach the president, but I also needed to ensure that its message was clear and well-executed. By that point, I was so bitter about my situation that I knew I couldn't be objective.

This is where knowing yourself comes into play along with having a network of friends and colleagues who have strengths that you are lacking. Throughout my entire professional career, I have rarely written a coherent and non-sassy email when I was annoyed or upset by a situation. Call it the emotional Pisces in me, but I knew from experience that if I write an email in an emotional state, I need to do one of two things: wait two to three days and re-read before sending it or seek out a friend who will counsel me on how to improve it. Both techniques have saved me a lot of social capital in the past. If you don't have these tips in your toolbox, be sure to remember them. Through trial and lots of error, I've learned the power of a big, fat, deep breath and a pause before pressing send.

It is also critical that within your friend group, you have at least one or two "ride or die" friends who are at your same level professionally. Typically, this type of relationship is reciprocal, where you step up greatly for your friends when they need professional support.

This evokes Newton's 3rd Law: For every action, there is an equal and opposite reaction. So, when you are in need, that friend steps in to provide a profession-al opinion, coaching, or a quick talk off a ledge. A few of my close friends fit these criteria. If you don't have an individual like this in your professional circle, it is important that you find one.

Work is better together, especially when you are in a traditionally marginalized group or are underrepresented in your office. Go to a networking event, find a colleague you trust at the office, and intentionally build a relationship with that person. Personal and professional relationships are a breath of fresh air when you are in a sea of work chaos.

That evening, I sent "the draft email of mush" followed by a quick text to two friends who are both business gurus, one in particular is a whiz at business communications. My friend KJ was on vacation with her husband in a beautiful beach setting. She received my text and took precious time out of her evening on the beach to talk with me about the email. She helped me define my main goal for the email and then coached me through rewriting the email based on what I hoped to accomplish.

Within the hour, she had helped me turn the mush into a professional and effective piece of communication. *This*, my friends, is a ride-or-die who is not only brilliant but also truly cares about my personal and professional well-being. Find yourself a KJ! They are great humans and are priceless.

1st Draft with KJ's feedback:

Hi Everyone,

Many of you have asked for an update so I thought I would send a quick email. My son was born in December. Even though he was born premature, he is doing well in the NICU. He is growing and passing his preemie milestones day by day. Many of the challenges that we discuss related to Black Maternal Health happened to me. Despite access to all of the resources, knowledge, and prevention mechanisms - the statistics hold true. All in all, I'm grateful that we are okay as we navigate new waters as NICU parents and the postpartum period.

Why am I back at work so soon:

- Similar to many NICU moms around the country, I am splitting my maternity leave (or saving the bulk of it) so that I can spend time with my son when he comes home from the NICU.
    - I took some time to recover from the delivery - I am currently returning to work for a few months - then I will be back on leave when he comes home from the NICU (hopefully in March).
    - This organization offers many buckets of leave to utilize outside of paternity leave (i.e. PTO, Sick, and Short-Term Disability) – however no one "plans" to have a preterm birth and most moms with children in the intensive care unit want to save options for when their child comes home. Navigating life after the NICU with a preemie can present its own set of new pathways. Many parents have had to do the same thing.
- A few weeks ago a TikTok went viral on this topic. Many news articles picked it up:
    - https://www.today.com/parents/moms/mom-shares-tiktok-returning-work-12-days-birth-rcna13075
    - NICU Mom Shares Sad TikTok About Maternity Leave – Motherly
- An example of a company that offers dedicated paid leave for NICU families (in addition to parental leave).
    - "This is one of the first companies we've heard of to provide dedicated leave to support NICU families. Keeping parents and NICU babies together during a hospital stay is critical to ensure the best possible outcomes for these families." —Keira Sorrells, Preemie Mom, Founder & Executive Director NICU Parent Network
    - https://newsroom.pinterest.com/en/post/pinterest-introduces-new-and-extended-parental-benefits-for-employees

Often those who bring attention to an issue do not get to experience the benefits of change or transformation, if they occur. Despite this, I hope this info spreads awareness for potential internal and external advocacy opportunities. Please feel free to pass this onto whoever may benefit from the update or information.

I am so grateful for your support during this time!
Warmest Regards, Sherenne

Changed the intro to a thank you which is more engaging to the reader.

Separated this section into bullets with a subheading for clarity.

Reformatted into bulleted sections with headings of "Maternity Leave" and "Broader Issues & Solution on Paternal Leave."

Highlighted the persuasion principle of "Commitment.»

Reframed the emotion in this section.

Highlighted the persuasion principle of "Social Proof."

Text with a bitter tone (AKA – Bitter Betty) reflected my true feelings but were removed to make the email digestible to a wider audience.

Modified the direct advocacy tone to a soft advocacy push with additional information.

Revised Version:

Hi Everyone,

Thank you to those who reached out with congratulations regarding the recent birth of my son. I've been adapting to the unique experience of being a NICU mom. In this email I'll share a personal update and some thoughts on the broader parental leave system.

Family Update:
- My son was born in December. Even though he was born a few months premature he is doing well in the NICU. He is growing and passing his preemie milestones day by day. See attached pics!
- Despite access to all the resources, knowledge, and prevention mechanisms - many statistics and experiences related to Black Maternal Health hold true. All in all, I'm grateful that we are okay as we navigate new waters as NICU parents and the postpartum period.

Maternity Leave:
- Like many NICU moms around the country, I am splitting my maternity leave (or saving the bulk of it) so I can spend time with my son when he comes home from the NICU.
- I took some time to recover from the delivery - I am currently returning to work for a few months (end of Jan-March) - then I will be back on leave when he comes home from the NICU (hopefully in March).
- Please email me at any time, I will be online afternoons and evenings with flexibility for important morning meetings.

Why navigate leave this way?
- This organization offers leave options outside of paternity leave (i.e. PTO, Sick, and Short Term Disability). However, one's original maternity leave plan is often altered with an unexpected preterm birth and a NICU stay. Many moms return to work shortly after birth and save leave options for when their baby comes home from the NICU. This is the situation for many parents without a leave option dedicated to a NICU experience and due to the expensive NICU costs.

Broader Issues & Solutions on Parental Leave and a NICU Experience
- A few weeks ago a TikTok went viral on this topic. Many news sources picked it up:
    - https://www.today.com/parents/moms/mom-shares-tiktok-returning-work-12-days-birth-rcna13075
    - NICU Mom Shares Sad TikTok About Maternity Leave - Motherly
- Here is an example of company that offers dedicated paid leave for NICU families (in addition to parental leave).
    - "This is one of the first companies we've heard of to provide dedicated leave to support NICU families." —Keira Sorrells, Preemie Mom, Founder & Executive Director NICU Parent Network
    - https://newsroom.pinterest.com/en/post/pinterest-introduces-new-and-extended-parental-benefits-for-employees

Overall - I am so grateful for your thoughts and congratulations during this time! We are excited for this new addition to our family. Thank you for your support as I navigate the postpartum period, caring for my son in NICU and working. I hope this clarifies my availability and brings awareness to potential internal and external advocacy opportunities.

Warmest Regards, Sherenne

Shorter and more engaging introduction.

Included a TLDR (for the millennial and Gen Z folks) otherwise known as a summary/overview sentence.

Started the conclusion with a tone of uplift instead of Bitter Betty.

Soft advocacy push and warm conclusion.

When reading the final email, note that first I took a few personal steps:

- Defined the goal or goal of the email for myself. I made it clear what I wanted to accomplish with this communication.

- Wrote a first draft but did not press send.

- Reached out to a friend whose strength complemented my weakness and asked for help.

Here are a few takeaways to help you craft your own email:

- Start with a summary of what will be discussed later in the email. Sometimes this is known as the executive summary. Or, more recently, it is called the "TLDR"—too long didn't read—section.

- Create sections of the email to chunk out different areas of thought that you want to communicate. Use subheadings to provide clarity for the reader.

- Include clear principles of persuasion and influence without being overt. There are "social proof and commitment" principles baked within my email.

- Zoom out on the emotion. Get rid of Bitter Betty if she shows up in the email. Revise it so that your words are more objective and informative.

- Consider using an indirect advocacy approach instead of a direct approach. This will depend on the most effective form of communication at the organization you are writing to.

- End the email on an upswing. A positive tone at the end of an email may prompt the reader to be more actionable. Include any relevant next steps.

I stayed up until 4 a.m. working on my email to make sure that all these components were included and that the tone and spelling were just right. The next morning, I sent the email to senior leadership on my team, the Chief Medical Officer (my boss), and the Chief Diversity Officer, hoping that it would eventually make its way up to the president.

I worked for the next two to three weeks and heard nothing. To say I was bitter was an understatement. I was also extremely exhausted, recovering from birth, and juggling doctors while visiting my baby in the NICU. I was barely functioning at work. During a weekly check-in, I spoke with my boss about the situation and the email. She mentioned that she was actively advocating for me in senior leadership meetings. I also connected with the Chief Diversity Officer who empathized with my situation and said that she heard something but was unsure about specifics.

During times like these, we put on a brave face and keep showing up for work. So, this is what I did during two of the most challenging months of my personal and professional life. The irony of my situation was overwhelming. Here I was the health equity lead at the largest maternal and child health advocacy organization in the country. I had just experienced what we are trying to eradicate in our company mission. I have a baby in the NICU, and I am working. This was a hard pill to swallow. *Geez, they really don't care*, I thought one afternoon while contemplating my exit from the organization.

Three weeks later, I skipped a monthly all-staff call because I was tired, bitter, sad, and so incredibly disappointed. During that hour, my cell phone blew up with texts from colleagues.

Sherenne, did you have something to do with this?

Oh wow, this is amazing, Sherenne, I'm so happy for you.

Wow finally, it's crazy that we did not have this before.

Very confused, I logged on to the staff call to hear the end of the president's announcement. She said that effective immediately, the organization would offer an additional four weeks of paid family leave to any family with a baby in the NICU—on top of the paid family leave already provided.

A huge smile appeared on my face and I immediately started to cry. I could not believe it! Now I could spend time with my baby while he was in the hospital without having to work. I felt my entire body exhale as if someone let the air out of the balloon of stress, worry, and difficulty that I was carrying.

Then it hit me. The "effective immediately" clause meant that leadership did this because of MY email.

They wanted ME to take advantage of the NICU leave that I had advocated for. *Holy Sh*t*, I thought, *I just managed to change a $100M organization with one email!*

My heart exploded with a ton of gratitude, joy, and a waterfall of relief. I was elated. I could have floated away when I realized this. I was overjoyed that they did not wait. The organization acted immediately and decided to' pioneer an uncommon and much-needed policy for NICU families. I was ecstatic that all families working for this organization, and hopefully others after me will have the same opportunity for paid family NICU leave, on top of the already provided paid family leave. I immediately texted my husband, mom, and the two friends who helped with the email. They were all overjoyed and very proud of what we had accomplished.

Logging off from my computer and spending those extra four weeks of paid leave with my son in the NICU were priceless. My mind and body had a moment to heal while I continued to spend time with him in the hospital and prepare for him to come home. Euphoria is what I felt every day that I had an opportunity to reshape the beginning of my motherhood journey with support from my job. It ended like a beautiful Hallmark movie with all the warm fuzzies, triumphs, and annoyingly positive storybook scenes that we see in those movies. I am grateful that today my son is healthy and thriving.

When personal and professional worlds collide, it is hard to keep a foot in both worlds as you navigate a truly difficult time. One's ability to multitask, take care of their physical and emotional health, perform adequately at work, and be present in their personal situation is like walking on a tightrope in a circus. I was ineffective at being everything to everyone – as most of us are. At one point though, there was an opening. A moment in time when I could have asked my boss to pass on a verbal message to leadership about my whereabouts. A moment where I could have swallowed my rage, bypassed my disappointment, and just accepted that "this is the way it is" for families like mine.

But I couldn't. Not with this situation. I could not let this issue slide by. Something deep inside me needed to say or do something, fully aware of the professional risks. In the midst of all of the chaos and difficulty, I acted on my intuition and wrote an email. I knew it was risky, but I asked for help with the email and used internal advocates to help me push it up the ladder. I influenced one of the oldest non-profits to change a critical policy for its employees because I acted on my intuition, found the courage to be brave, and spoke up strategically using lessons from prior work experiences. At the end of the day, I did not ignore that feeling in my gut.

Your gut, your intuition, your divine message will always be your best guide in the workplace. It is the most crucial muscle you can build and nurture in your professional career. It can be hard to discern intuition when anxiety and fear get in the way. But you must find a way to tap into it. Read a book, find a coach, talk to a friend, treat your anxiety, get quiet, go for a walk, and figure out how to tap into that little voice in your head or your heart. It will give you the best advice based on all the lessons you have learned in the past. It will direct you to create or act in alignment with your own best interest, time and time again.

I will never know the exact reason why the leadership at this well-known non-profit said "yes" to my email and changed their policy. I can speculate that the email included convincing persuasion principles of commitment and social proof. I can speculate that they liked me as a person, or they felt very sorry for me. I can assume that I built up enough social capital and trust for my email to stick. Or perhaps the leadership had been unaware of their blind spot in the organization and acted quickly out of embarrassment. I can speculate that they did it because it was the right thing to do as an organization working in maternal and child health.

At the end of the day, the reason they chose to say yes matters less than the journey I took through the ups and downs of my professional career. That path led me to trust my intuition, speak up, ask for help, navigate risks, and ultimately make meaningful changes to a well-known national institution for social good. As cliché as it sounds, the journey truly is the destination.

A journey that led me to change a $100M organization with one email and leave a legacy for all employees.

Sometimes you need a little courage, self-awareness, a kind friend, and a history of navigating professional roller coasters to write a life-changing email.

10

Where do we go from here?

So, how do you capture that accomplishment on a resume? How do you condense into one bullet, or even a series of bullets, that you achieved something remarkable, left a lasting legacy, and became a trailblazer for an important cause? More importantly, how do you express that the last two decades were spent learning, growing, falling on your face, and picking yourself up to finally reach both a personal and professional peak? Honestly, I have no idea.

Sure, I could have given myself a pat on the back, celebrated with family, or waited for someone else to acknowledge the accomplishment. But that afternoon, when I sat down to work on my resume and sat there stuck for hours, it finally came to me—I had to share that journey with you. I knew that anyone would be eager to read the email that changed a $100M organization. But now you are aware of what was behind the email—the person, the passion, the resilience, the emotion, and the strategy.

You now know that overcoming adversity is something that underrepresented people (or who feel "othered" or "less than") in professional life must do time and time again. Any desire or action to influence change is a risk that has the potential to bring a (sometimes unwelcome) spotlight to our being, our cause, and our voice. Our efforts can be successful, a complete failure, or just lead to more of the same. Underrepresented people in professional spaces have no choice but to act with an intentional level of strategy, agility, and tact when working within the nuances of the workplace.

All the nuggets of wisdom from my rollercoaster journey are now yours. Principles such as building trust and credibility, navigating likability and authenticity, investing in social capital, promoting your accomplishments, creating boundaries during a personal crisis, and managing stress responses can help you grow as a professional and add wonderful tools to your toolbox.

Understand how these dynamics play out in your professional environment. Use them like pieces on a chess board.

With new tools in your toolbox, you can navigate tricky professional situations, curate your career, and take strategic risks, all at the same time. It is a muscle that can be built up over time. Let go of what is holding you back and release the anxiety, fear, and worry. Tap into your intuition, find courage, and act. Take a calculated risk and let the cards fall as they may.

When you take the time to reflect and learn about your professional experiences, the possibilities are endless. I felt a whole host of emotions writing this book—joy, happiness, relief, and re-triggered trauma. But in the end, looking back is a powerful exercise. Those moments of success and difficult lessons in your past are gems to help you figure out the fabric of who you are, where you've been, and what impact you truly desire to make personally or professionally.

So, what will you do the next time that little voice in your head is angry or frustrated at a workplace injustice? What will you do when you see something is unfair and want to make a difference? Will you step up?

Will you get creative and figure out a way to overcome the lack of support or resources to move forward? Will you let the feeling of powerlessness overtake you and stop you from doing something? You have just read a myriad of stories and strategies to help you get through that moment the next time it occurs.

I have always said that with big problems, you don't have to do everything, but you can do something. We all have the power to do something. You may not be a CEO, VP, or a manager. However, we can all affect change in our professional lives in some way. Cornel West said, "We must not confuse success with greatness. Success is being in a position of authority, power, and influence. Greatness is what you do with it." All of us have some level of authority, power, or influence in our jobs, our work life, or in our organizations. My question is, how will you use that authority, power, or influence to do something with a positive impact?

With stitches in my abdomen from just delivering a baby and a newborn in the hospital, I chose to act. I took a risk and it stuck. It ended up changing a $100M organization and leaving a legacy for all NICU families that pass through that organization. You, too, can influence change for the good of yourself, others, and your workplace. Now tap deep within, roll up your sleeves, lean on others, find your voice, and go!

...and don't forget to tell others about it. *wink*

Acknowledgements

I have to start by first thanking my incredibly supportive husband, Rock. From encouraging me to write a life-changing email, to giving me countless high fives *wink*, and providing ongoing advice throughout the journey to write my first book. Thank you so very much, love.

Thank you to my mom, Linda, and sisters, Sharlene and Clarissa, for your endless support throughout the ups and downs of my personal and professional life. You all are my foundation.

To my ride-or-die tribe of girlfriends, Andrea, Fatimah, Jacqui, Kate, Shelley, Akilah, and April - Your love, support, sisterly advice, raw honesty, workplace insight, and many happy hours have helped me ride the rollercoasters in this book with grace and class.

Toni, my coach and sister from another mister. Thank you for guiding me during this book-writing journey, putting up with my panic calls, and seeing the magic in me that I did not have the courage to see.

Thank you to Fatimah, Arianne, Jacqui, and Kate, for reading early drafts of the book. Your eyes helped transform this work. Additional thanks to my editors Lydia, Susanna, and Michelle for your skills, wisdom, and insight.

Thank you, Dad, for always reminding me not to work too hard and to slow down. I love and miss you.

IMG, my heartbeat, je t'aime.